Maureen Susan Birkett

To God Be The Glory

A Book of Christian Poetry

Outskirts Press, Inc.
Denver, Colorado

This is a work of fiction. The events and characters described herein are imaginary and are not intended to refer to specific places or living persons. The opinions expressed in this manuscript are solely the opinions of the author and do not represent the opinions or thoughts of the publisher.

To God Be The Glory
A Book of Christian Poetry
All Rights Reserved.
Copyright © 2008 Maureen Susan Birkett
V3.0R1.0

Cover Photo © 2008 JupiterImages Corporation. All rights reserved - used with permission.

This book may not be reproduced, transmitted, or stored in whole or in part by any means, including graphic, electronic, or mechanical without the express written consent of the publisher except in the case of brief quotations embodied in critical articles and reviews.

Outskirts Press, Inc.
http://www.outskirtspress.com

ISBN: 978-1-4327-1961-6

Outskirts Press and the "OP" logo are trademarks belonging to Outskirts Press, Inc.

PRINTED IN THE UNITED STATES OF AMERICA

Dedication

This book is being dedicated first and foremost to "The Glory and Honor of God".

Secondly, this book is being dedicated to a very special person who encouraged me to start writing poetry again after many years of not writing, Pastor James L. Garner Jr.

Thirdly, I would like to dedicate this book to my loving family: my husband, Rich; my daughters: Kimberly and Tara Ann and my granddaughters: Hailey-Marie and Katelyn.

I would like to thank some very special people who helped me in compiling some of my best work: Rosemary L. Moore, Marcia Archibald, Karen Pawlowski and Katherine Patluneas.

Last, but not least, I would like to especially thank my congregation. The people of Scottsville have given me confidence and words of encouragement that helped make this book a reality.

Table of Contents

CREATION

God Is In	3
A Work of Art	4
Winter to Spring	5
New Life	6
Spring Brings Life	7
Spring Glory	8
Autumn, God's Handiwork	9
Autumn Creation	10

GOD'S CHARACTER

God Reaches Out	13
Lord I Praise You	14
Blessings	15
Treasures From God	16
My Lord, My Life	17
Where is God?	18
And It Was So	19
Gifts From God	20
From This Day Forth	21
Great Shepherd	22
God is There	23

My Prayer	24
Through It All	25
He's There	26
An Angel	27
Blessings of Enrichment	28
Jesus	29
Jesus, The Great Physician	30
The Light	31
Of The Spirit	32
Lord, You Take My Breath Away	33
Listen	34

THE CHRISTIAN LIFE

Evil In Our Times	37
It Was All In God's Plan	38
The Dance	39
Thank You Lord	41
A Fire Inside	42
Prayer Can	43
What Can I Give?	44
God's Voice	45
Take Me Away	47
Turning To God	48
I Am A Servant	49
A Servant's Heart	50
The Christ In Me	51
My Calling	52
Answered Prayer	53
Peace God's Plan	55
Women of Mission	56
A Life Change	57
Lord, Thy Will Be Done	58
Treasures In Heaven	59

A Heart For Christ	60
Open My Heart	61
A Relationship With God	62
Christian Love	64
Can You Drink?	65
Servanthood	66
Pay It Forward	67
Find Your Passion	68
A Calling To Care	69

JESUS' BIRTH AND ETERNAL LIFE

He Came To Earth	73
Prince Of Peace	74
Christmas After Christmas	76
The Light Of Christ	78
Christmas Joy	79
Jesus' Birth	80
God Sent	81
Jesus Is Born	82
A Dark Road To Life	83
Eastertide	85
King of Kings	86

SPECIAL OCCASIONS

Happy Mother's Day	89
Mother, Did You Know?	90
Mother/Child	91
We Are Proud	92
The Relationship	94
You're Part Of Me	95

A Shared Union	96
Words Never Spoken	97
Open Us To Music	98
Service In The Lord	99

CREATION

God Is In

God is in the flower,
God is in the rain.

God is in the mountains,
Throughout the earth's terrain.

God is in the starry skies,
He out-shines the brightest star.

God is all around you,
No matter where you are.

God is there in darkness,
As a guiding light.

God is there beside you,
Throughout every plight.

God fills the earth with beauty,
He is in everything.

His mighty hand it touches,
And the earth explodes in spring!

A Work of Art

Sweet are the morning flowers,
That shimmer in the dew.

All things bright and beautiful,
To start a day, anew.

Soft is the sunlit morning,
Brightening up my day,

Gentle is the tender breeze,
That follows on my way.

Quiet is the whisper
Of the Spirit of my heart.

Oh Lord, you are in all of these,
They are your work of art.

Winter to Spring

The deadly cold of winter,
Has finally lost its sting.

Open the doors and windows,
To the beauty, that is spring.

The fields green, like carpets,
Cover an earth of clay,

And all the snows of winter,
Have finally passed away.

The flowers fill our world with color,
There's a sweetness in the breeze.

Everything is greening,
Birds are nesting in the trees.

The beauty of "God's Creation",
An overwhelming sense of wonder.

The creation of new life,
For all mankind to ponder!

New Life

As the gentleness of a spring breeze,
Blows a balm of warmth against my face,
I breathe the Spirit into my soul.

As a rainbow of colors and beauty,
Dance around me and encircle my being,
I drench myself in the Lord's gifts of creation.

As I breathe the sweetness of the flowers,
On the hillside, I surrender myself to God's Majesty.
My mind, body and soul become refreshed, renewed.

I Become Alive!

For all I need has been given to me.

Spring Brings Life

Quickly spring, come today
While cold and snows faded away

Come to me sweet birds of song,
With sweetest melodies, sing along.

Grow for me green, green grass,
Carpeting hills and valley alas.
Clothe the green with bright-colored flowers,
To linger, a fragrance of sweetness for hours.

Dew dances on flowers, in early morning light,
The explosion of spring is a glorious sight!

Spring Glory

A babbling brook,
Is my delight.
A breath of spring,
A bird takes flight.

The warmth of the sun,
Upon my face,
Awestruck by God,
Majestic Grace!

The golden sun,
The greening grass,
The explosion of spring,
Unfolding fast.

The budding earth,
And every flower,
The brightest colors,
Fill our hour.

Celebration of Spring,
The Creation Story,
Giving Praise to the Lord,
Lifting God in Glory!

Autumn, God's Handiwork

When leaves of green, become red and gold,
And earth reveals treasures untold.

When the burning hearth fills the cool, crisp air,
And children of God are warmed in His care.

The harvest moon shines a bright orange haze,
And time gives way to shorter days.

Gods' treasures of autumn now fill the land,
The handiwork of God, the touch of His hand.

Autumn Creation

Gentle drifting whirls of wind,
Leaves of colors swirl within.

Shimmering gold, orange and red,
A sea of trees, that lies ahead.

The amazing paintbrush of God's hand.
Has danced across this autumn land.

With leaves orange, red and gold,
The Creator's beauty we behold.

And in awe we thank, thee above,
For this creation designed with Love!

GOD'S CHARACTER

God Reaches Out

I'll reach across the Great Divide.
Beyond the walls of despair.

I'll extend a hand of Peace,
To reach you there.

I'll crush the vale of darkness,
If you will speak, "Come In".

I will wipe away a past of hurts,
And wash away the sin.

I will bless you, as you turn to me.
You will rise anew.

Out of the dark of shadows,
A new strength will fill you.

You will be fed and nourished,
As on God's Holy Word.

And a voice will speak to you,
"It's Me, your God you heard."

Lord I Praise You

Lord, I praise You from morning till night,
You made all creation, pleasant in sight.

Lord, I praise You, day after day,
For green covered hills, as we travel our way.

Lord, I praise You, for love so divine,
A Love sent from heaven, for yours and for mine.

Lord, I praise You, for gifts freely given,
May they glorify You, in the life we're livin'

Lord, I praise You, for the grace, that is You,
And Your goodness that shines in the things we do.

Lord, I will praise You for all of my days,
Eternally, always singing Your praise.

Blessings

Tender blessings from above,
First of all our Father's Love.

Precious blessings our Lord gives,
To everyone of us who lives.

A blessing of our children fair,
The loving arms of those who care.

The blessing of a single day,
That brings us hope, as we humbly pray.

The blessing of Christ, God's only Son,
Who died for us, when all was done.

These are the blessings we treasure forever,
Let us remember, forgetting them, never.

Treasures From God

We Thank You,
Our Heavenly Father above,
For Your unfailing grace,
And infinite love.

With guidance and encouragement,
You enfold me each day,
Help me, grow and prosper,
As I follow Your way.

Oh, giver of gifts,
And all of life's pleasures,
None can surpass,
"Gods Love" the true treasure.

My Lord, My Life

You are my protector,
In You, I find my shelter,
From life's raging storms.

You restore and renew me daily,
In Your arms I find my rest,
When I am weary.

You are the great healer,
In You I find strength,
As You enfold me.

You are my provider,
You tend to my needs,
And clothe me with compassion.

You are my Lord,
My Life, My Hope,
Sustainer of Life.

In You I find all I need!

Where is God?

Where is God?
I can not see Him,
But, all nature sings of His greatness and glory.

Where is God?
I can not hear Him,
But, if His word is written in your heart
It will reverberate through eternity.

Where is God?
I can not taste Him,
But, the sweetness of His Compassion and
Faithfulness flow through my life.

Where is God?
I can not smell Him,
But, the fragrance of His creation,
Fills the earth.

Where is God?
I can not touch Him.
But, through the love of others,
He reaches out and holds me close.

Where is God?
Don't you know?
He's inside you, beside you,
Wherever you go!

And It Was So

God said, Learn to pray.
And it was so.

God said, turn away from evil.
And it was so.

God said, I will be with you.
And it was so.

God said, follow my commands.
And it was so.

God said, worship only me.
And it was so.

God said, meditate on my word.
And it was so.

God said, care for others.
And it was so.

God said, "My Will Be Done".
And it was so.

Gifts From God

Gracious Lord, my Father,
Giver of the abundant life,

You who remain consoler,
Throughout our daily strife,

Giver of abundant harvest,
Giver of loving grace,

Giver of strength and courage,
In all that we must face.

For the gifts, our Lord bestowed,
Upon us all this day,

Let us show our Thankfulness,
As we humbly bow to pray.
Amen.

From This Day Forth

Rest on me,
Fill me
With your Spirit.

Draw me close,
Burn within me,
From the start.

Cleanse me,
Give me Peace,
Walk with me.

Be ever-present,
Guiding me,
Close within my heart.

Great Shepherd

Great shepherd, guide them,
The great and the small,
From the time they are little,
Keep them from the fall.

Give them strength,
Give them wisdom,
As they go on their way,
Watchfully guide them,
Day after day.

Bring them Your comfort,
Your warmth and Your Love,
Enfold them in peace,
As You watch from above.

And when they grow older,
May they follow Your plan,
With the great shepherd, Jesus,
As they walk hand in hand.

God Is There

In times of trouble, I am there,

Your thoughts and prayers, With you I share.

When you worry, Though you naught.

I'm there, That's what I've taught.

You may be hurting, And no longer know

I'm there with love, To guide you so

Times may be tough, I'll share your pain,

For I'm in you, I'll never wane.

My Prayer

Lord heal me,
For I am hurting.

Repair me,
For I am broken.

Remold me,
And make me new.

Replenish me,
With a healing Spirit.

Draw me,
Into oneness with You.

Immerse me,
In Your words.

Fill me,
With faith and understanding.

Create in me,
Your work of art.

Through It All

Though you stand,
At the threshold,
Of darkness and despair.

Fear Not!
The Lord is with you,
Keeping you in His care.

He takes your hand.
And walks with you.
His comfort will not cease.

Surrender to Him fully,
And know the gift of Peace.

For God has sent us Jesus,
To walk the path of life.

And He is always with us,
Throughout each daily strife.

If to Him you surrender,
Your problems still remain,
But, Jesus will be with you,
To help and ease the pain!

He's There

He's there every morning,
He's there every night.

He's there through the tough times,
To make things all right.

He's in you, beside you,
He can't be mistaken.

For when He's near you,
Your life can't be shaken.

Faithful, compassionate,
Giver of life,

Friend of man throughout
Daily Strife.

An Angel

God sent me an Angel,
To watch over me today.
I didn't know my Angel,
Would help me when I pray.

God sent me an Angel,
To help me get things done.
I didn't know that Angels,
Could be kind of fun.

God sent me an Angel,
To tuck me in just right,
And now my Guardian Angel,
Works hard, all through the night.

God sent me an Angel,
To watch over me with care.
All around me is God's presence,
I'm Thankful, He is there!

Blessings of Enrichment

Tender is the breeze,
That gently caresses the cheek,

Calm is the wind,
In which we hear God speak.

Warming is the sun,
As it's filtered by the shade,

Magnificent creation,
All His hands have made.

Refreshing is the summer rain,
That cleanses all the earth.

Washing away our sinfulness,
Giving us rebirth.

Enriched becomes the soil,
And the trees and flowers grow.

Enriched become our lives,
In living God's word, we know.

For all the tender blessings,
Bestowed from up above,

They become so meaningless,
If we know, nothing of God's Love!

Jesus

Jesus, the teacher,
Jesus, the man,
Jesus, sent to fulfill God's Plan.

Jesus, the healer,
Our Comforter, our Hope.
Jesus, our Strength, teach us to cope.

Jesus our Deliverer,
The sinners we be,
Our step on the walk,
To Eternity.

Jesus, the help of the souls,
That be lost,
Jesus, the Servant who gave at
Great cost.

All praise to God,
For the grace He bestowed,
Who brought us salvation,
Through the Jesus we know.

Jesus, The Great Physician

Jesus, You are the Great Physician,
    Heal my broken body.

Jesus, You are the Great Physician,
    Heal my tormented mind.

Jesus, You are the Great Physician,
    Heal my broken heart.

Jesus, You are the Great Physician,
    Heal my broken Spirit.

Jesus, You are the Great Physician,
    Heal my restless soul!

The Light

The light shone, but there was much darkness;

The light was warm, but the world was cold.

The light gave direction, but they were still searching.

The light broke the darkness, they were no longer alone.

The light blanketed the world, hearts started melting.

It lighted a pathway to Peace and Goodwill.

It Illumined the soul!

Of The Spirit

Peace of the Spirit
Breathe on my soul.
Enter my heart,
And make me whole.

Truth of the Spirit
Speak to my heart,
Make me complete,
Of You a part.

Light of the Spirit
Illumine the way,
So I will follow,
Day by Day.

Love of the Spirit
My heart knows,
In Christian Love,
My heart overflows.

Lord, You Take My Breath Away

Lord, You take my breath away,
There's awe in each creation,
That fills a single day,
And You take my breath away.

Lord, majestic is Your Name,
I praise in heaven and earth,
You're the miracle of Life,
Celebrated at the birth.

Lord, Creation sings your song,
As the mountains tower trees,
As the waves of tide grow strong,
And Your hand, it rocks the seas.

Lord, The fragrant flower is sweet,
Beauty blossoms all around,
As Your sweetness fills the air,
And soft petals touch the ground.

There's the lush enfolds of green,
As I lie upon the ground,
And a spray of wildflowers,
That dances all around.

Lord, You take my breath away,
There's awe in each creation,
That fills a single day.
And You take my breath away!

Listen

Listen, I'm speaking.
You come to me and you are in my presence.

Listen, I hush the worldly distractions,
Now you will hear my voice.

Listen, My words are your message
Of hope, comfort, strength and sustenance.

Listen, Become connected.
Your life will be made new!

THE
CHRISTIAN LIFE

Evil in Our Times

We are in dark times,
But, our Lord calls us!

We are living in fear,
But, we hear "Fear Not!"

We seek revenge,
But, find it has no place in our hearts!

We are fighting evil,
But God is on the side of the righteous!

We feel threatened,
But the Lord is by our side!

We fear the End,
But, we have Eternal Life!

We see no justice,
The final Judgement Day
Is in the Lord's hands!

It Was All In God's Plan

I fell and suffered
Bruises and sprains,
No broken bones,
I was able to walk away.
It was all in God's Plan.

I was in a serious car accident,
My car was totaled,
I suffered bruises and debilitating pain.
I learned to cope and move on.
By drawing closer to the Lord.
It was all in God's Plan.

I found a lump,
It was cancerous,
Love and Support surrounded me,
I am blessed,..I am a survivor,
It was all in God's Plan.

Our lives (as we knew them) were crumbling
We lost our jobs,
We lost our home,
We Gained a Life with the Lord,
It was all in God's Plan!

*Our journey through life may be racked with suffering,
But to live with Christ will be our Gain!

The Dance

I danced with the devil,
But, the pain was great.

He tore at my heart,
He would not dissipate.

I cried to the Lord,
Free me from his clutch.

There was a great struggle,
For my soul, the pain was much.

God was there beside me,
He was there all along.

I just needed to reach up,
I just needed to be strong.

My God, He won the battle,
He helped me take a stand.

Against the Evil One,
And now I'm in God's hands.

I walk with God and He with me,
From morning until night.

He never leaves my side,
Regardless of the plight.

He has filled me with His Spirit,
And completely changed my life.

I'm rest assured in his abiding Love,
Throughout my daily strife.

Oh Father, God in Heaven,
I Gratefully lift my praise,
And with You Lord I promise,
To walk with You always!

You are my Life! My Light! My Salvation!

Thank You Lord

Thank you Lord,
For morning and night.

The sun upon rising,
The moon and stars bright.

Thank You, for a breath of fresh air,
And above all else, The love that we share.

And I thank You for Your amazing Unconditional Love,
Which You pour down upon us, from heaven above.

Thank You, for all the gifts You bestow,
May I use them in service to You, as I grow.

Thank You for Your gentleness and tender loving care,
I can count on You, and I know You are there.

As I continue through life, on my way,
Be ever in my mind and my heart as I pray.

Make me an example in all that I do.
In the service of loving devotion to You.

A Fire Inside

Ignite a spark within my heart,
Fan the embers, flames will start.

Deepening my faith a fire will burn,
Consuming me through all I learn.

His will, though struggles come to be,
As He burns a fire inside of me.

Prayer Can

If I but learn a discipline, Just one, throughout my strife.

It would be the discipline, Of a devout prayerful life.

For prayer can serve, As comfort,

Or ease the torment of pain.

Prayer can take you from darkness,

And bring you to the light again.

Prayer can soothe a broken heart,

A soul, whom would seem lost.

Prayer can bridge a relationship,

Thanks to Christ upon the cross.

What Can I Give?

Lord You are calling,
Where should I go?

Into a life,
I really don't know?

In faith let me step out,
And discover my gift.

Seeking Christian companionship,
Giving a spiritual lift.

Should I share my faith,
Imitate Christ in my Living?

Should I be open,
Caring and Giving?

Am I to sing praise,
Or am I to teach?

Am I to visit the sick,
Or give a community speech?

Uncharted water, may lie ahead,
But through the power of the Spirit,
We all will be led!

God's Voice

Lord, Did you know,
I need to talk?

I'm having trouble,
With my walk.

The path I'm on,
Is filled with choices.

It's hard to distinguish,
The different voices.

There is my own voice,
That wants my way.

There's another voice,
Saying, "It's Okay!"

Then there's a voice,
That whispers through trees.

Saying, "Follow me, your Lord
You must please."

The Voice says:
"Just listen and stay in touch."

"For you, my dear child,
My Love is much."

"I'll guide you, instruct you,
Let joy fill your day."

"In my word, I'll direct you
And, We'll talk as you pray."

"And when the time comes
To make the right choices."

"Mine will be, the words,
And no other voices"

Take Me Away

Let me draw close to You.

Take Me Away,
Where I can sit, just sit,
In Your presence.

Take Me Away ,
To the Mountain Top.

Shelter Me, beneath Your wing.

As You, Take Me Away,
And draw me close!

Turning to God

Do not give up,
In your despair.

Reach out to God,
He's standing there.

Do not lose hope,
At any cost.

God's there to help,
When all seems lost.

Fall to your knees,
Pour out your heart.

Blessings upon blessings,
God will impart.

Circumstances may not change,
But the you inside, will rearrange.
And all the things you could not bear,
Are less a burden, when God is there!

I Am A Servant

As in service,
To the Lord

May I commit,
To others.

Give me a heart,
Of service Lord.

To care for and Help,
My brothers.

Help me strive,
In all I do.

And walk,
In your Godly way.

As an imitator,
Of the Lord,

In all I do,
And say.

A Servant's Heart

Give me Lord.
A thankful heart,
As I bow my head in prayer.

Give me Lord.
A giving heart,
Showing others that I care.

Give me Lord.
A caring heart,
To share, a piece of me.

Give me Lord.
A peaceful heart,
And life will blissful be.

Give me Lord.
A heart for You,
As I lift Your praise in song.

Give me Lord.
A thankful heart,
You bless my whole life long.

The Christ In Me

I look upon the sick, the poor,
The hurting, with compassion.

I am Jesus' eyes!

I reach out with healing words,
Prayers and touch.

I am Jesus' hands!

I travel to carry the Good News,
To those who are lost and alone.

I am Jesus' feet!

I speak words of Praise and Thanks,
To God for His "Unconditional Love".

I am Jesus' mouth!

I am filled with the Peace, Joy and
The Love of Christ!

I have Jesus' Heart!

My Calling

Lord, You know where I am needed,
You know that I do care.

Wherever You decide to send me,
I know You'll lead me there.

You'll give me strength and courage,
You'll send me on my way.

But, You'll be there to guide me,
Walking together day by day.

If it be feeding the hungry,
Or comforting the poor.

May I spread joy of You, Lord,
And desire to do more.

I strive to do Your will, Oh Lord,
In faith and love endure.

For all my life, I choose to give,
To service, Evermore!

Answered Prayer

It's crashing in around me.
I feel inadequate, tired,
Useless, weak, not capable.

I close my eyes,
I escape,
No more clutter,
No more chores.

I pray,
Bring me peace,
In the midst of despair,
Over the things,
I cannot do.

Bring me help,
I need strength,
I need You Lord.

If it be Your will,
Bring me healing.
I cannot go on
Without You!

The Lord says:
I have given you all you need
I'm your Peace,
In prayer you find Me.

I have given you help
Family, friends, the church,
Learn to reach out.

I am your strength.
I have been with you,
Every step of the way.

I have offered you healing.
Through acceptance and spiritual growth,
With a dependency upon Me!

Peace God's Plan

When brothers all walk hand in hand,
And people pray throughout our land,
Then in Peace, we'll take our stand,
And all will follow God's Great Plan.

Then with a guiding divine grace,
The Lord will heal the Human Race,
A world of Peace in which we'd live,
With all our Praise to God we'd give.

Who spared the lives of those untold,
And turned us from our ways of old.

As One, we all will celebrate,
A God with power to recreate,
And set the hearts and spirits free,
To dwell in Peace eternally.

Women of Mission

Women of Mission,
Work hand and hand,

Throughout this world,
Across this land.

Freely giving,
To all in need,
With our blessings,
And God speed.

Examples of Christ,
Compassion and giving,
Honoring life,
Giving value to living!

A Life Change

My Life is filled.
With things to do.

Oh, Lord let me,
Make time for You.

My life is filled,
Taken control.

I must surrender,
My heart and soul.

I need to find,
Some time to rest.

And reflect on You,
As I return with zest.

The Spiritual fire may
Be burning low,

Seeking God's guidance,
A brilliance will glow.

A Life of Peace,
Will be with me,

As I seek His will,
Eternally!

Lord, Thy Will Be done

Lord in me, thy will be done,
From the morning dew till evening sun.

Following Your ways, may I prepare,
With Love and compassion to be there.

I'll touch the lives I see each day,
And they'll know that God has passed their way.

With joyful hearts they will profess,
The Lord is revealed, never the less.

He may seem to perform in smallish ways.
But, lives have transformed to better days.

So, though His will is not yet known,
He's our companion, we're not alone.

My trust will abound and faith will be,
In God's time He'll reveal to me!

Treasures In Heaven

Fast from this world,
Be heavenly directed,

Be God focused,
In Him be protected.

Cast aside,
All worldly pleasures,
Serving your Lord,
Find true treasures.

Riches of the world,
May be at your door,

They overflow,
You just want more.

They don't last forever,
Rust and mold destroy,

Then turning to God,
We must employ,

"Treasures in heaven,
Your hearts must hold,

Far greater than silver,
And finer than gold."

A Heart for Christ

I search my heart,
For then I see,
That Christ, He dwells,
Inside of me.

"Care for my people",
The sick, and the poor,
My heart cries out,
"I must do more!"

Care for the hurting,
The lonely, the lost,
Filling their needs,
Love at no cost.

Touch hearts full of sorrow,
Heal lives that are broken,
Guiding hearts toward Christ,
Finding "Joy" as the token.

Open My Heart

Lord, open my heart,
Bring forth my inner most self.

Bring forth a part,
That's hid on the shelf.

Create a new bond,
That I'll share with You,

Heartfelt I'll respond,
And You'll see me through.

Fill a void within me,
Replace the despair.

For there You will be,
My lifetime to share.

Oh, Thank Him above,
My Father of Grace.

Who opens me to Love,
And shows me my place.

Your Spirit is in me,
As it is Your will.

May Peace, Joy and Love be,
That of my heart's fill.

A Relationship With God

Lord, You've opened up my heart,
You've found this sacred space.

Lord, You've opened up my eyes,
To Your amazing grace.

The relationship I have with You,
Is my treasure here on earth.

I'm blessed to be a child of God,
You've given life value and worth.

You share my inner being,
As day-to-day I bear,

Without a spoken word,
There's a oneness that we share.

What amazes me most of all,
This I must confess.

Is the power of Your abiding love,
And undying faithfulness.

For nothing will come between us,
No matter what may be.

I know You'll never give up,
As You continue Your work in me.

You have placed within my heart,
A consuming desire, to burn,

As I continue on my journey,
My soul for You does yearn.

Lord You're always there for me,
So I'll make time for You.
And develop our relationship,
In all I say and do.

I'll meditate; I'll sing Your praise,
As I kneel in prayer each day.

I'll confess my every sin, Oh Lord,
I'll never turn away.

For I am truly grateful, Lord.
You play a vital part.
My Life, my love, my confidant,
The Light within my heart!

Christian Love

It's Love that shines
From within the heart,
That shows we're Christians,
From the start.

It's the little things,
We do and say.
That shows others,
There's a different way.

It's the way we share,
It's the way we care,

It's our knowing assurance,
God's always there.

It's the example of Christ,
We strive to portray,
As we seek guidance,
And direction each day.

So ask yourself,
Will my life do?
Does the Christian Love,
Shine through me too?

The answer to you,
Should be clear,
"Yes, The Love of Christ
Lives Here!"

Can You Drink?

Can you drink, the cup of Life?
Full of sorrows, and daily strife.

Laced with sweetness, full of flavor,
Found in moments, that we savor.

Can you live, a life of care,
Knowing God is always there?

Can you live, in thankful bliss?
Following Christ.
Remembering this:

Lift the cup,
As you prepare,
To drench in the fullness,
Of Godly care.

Hold the Cup,
Smell the sweetness,
Anticipate,
A new completeness.

Drink the cup,
Submit to the will,
A Godly Life,
The Lord fulfill!

Servanthood

Lord bring me to servanthood,
Show me the way.

Let me touch lives,
I encounter each day.

Help me surrender,
And give of my life.

In total commitment,
Through out daily strife.

Grow me in grace,
Compassion and love.
Prepare me and fit me,
For service above.

Pay It Forward

Do you find yourself…
Doing good for those who do good for you?

Why not pay it forward? Why not, just reach out?
Someone is in need…That's what it's about.

A kindness or a hand, may be all they need,
Unconditional Love in Action, Has planted God's seed.

Your action could be…What makes their day.
Maybe just a smile…Or a courtesy their way.

A gift of time…A lend of an ear.
A helping hand…A nourishing meal.

Shelter from a storm, To a passer by,
A heartfelt prayer…Or share a good cry.

Give hope, to the hopeless,
As you pour out God's Love.

Peace will descend upon you,
As a dove.

As you pay it forward,
Expect, not in return.

Great is your reward,
In all that you've learned.

Find Your Passion

Live your Life,
Find the real you.

Celebrate all the fun
In the things that you do.

Live your Passion,
As in excitement you're driven,
And you'll have a thirst,
For the Life you're livin'!

A Calling to Care

I'm hidden in loneliness,
In dark despair.

You did not visit me.
You were not there.

I lay abandoned on the streets of town.

I had no shelter, I lay on the ground.

The cans in the alleys, held my feast.

You could have fed me, a meal at least.

I lay sick in the cold, damp and rain.

How could you just ignore my pain?

For I am human, just like you.

And I need love, like we all do.

If goodness and mercy shown
to the least of these

Surely our Lord would be
very pleased.

No greater love,
could you have shown,

Than to care for one
of us, as if your own.

JESUS' BIRTH AND ETERNAL LIFE

He Came to Earth

Lord, You came to earth as one,
Who would know our hearts and minds,
Who would offer up His son,
For the Love of human kind.

And You taught Your people well,
As Your Son came down to earth,
The Great Sacrificial Love.
Gave our lives value and worth.

Jesus taught us how to pray,
And taught us how to Love,
And told us of a Father.
Who cared from heaven above.

Prince of Peace

Don't get all caught up,
In the Holiday Stressing,
What's it all about?
Why all so pressing?

For the true Joy of the Season,
Will not be found in a store,
It's found in a manger,
Where we begin to explore!

Meditate on the babe
In the manger so fair,
With Mother and Father,
And all that were there.

The shepherds, the angels,
The sheep and the cow,
What a glorious presence,
Jesus, here now!

The Gift that was hidden,
In the Peace of the night,
Is well worth the discovery,
For setting hearts right.

As the Prince of Peace enters,
God's symbol of Love,
We open our hearts,
To His life giving Love.

Then we discover the reason,
For True celebration,
A Savior is born,
There is true Jubilation!

Christmas After Christmas

After all the glitter,
Decoration and the lights,

After all the gifts and bows,
And parties that delight,

After all the hustle,
And the bustle of the Season.

Did you ever stop and pause,
Did it have rhyme or reason?

Why all the frazzle?
Why all the stress?

Was this what Christmas should be?
Was Christmas at its best?

The simplicity of Christmas
The Christmas of the past.

The babe of the manger,
A Peace and Joy that last.

The shining Love of Jesus Christ,
The darkness has been broken.

Reflections of a Father's Love,
Our first Christmas as a token.

But you say "It's over!"
"For me it seems too late."

But, Christmas should live in our hearts,
Beyond a certain date.

The Joy found Christmas morning,
God's gift to us that day

Should ring throughout eternity,
And dwell within our hearts to stay!

The Light of Christ

The Light came into darkness,
To give us the Hope of Peace.

The Light came into darkness,
So fighting and wars might cease.

The Light came into darkness,
A manifestation of Love.

The Light came into darkness,
A gift sent from above.

The Light came into darkness,
To fill us and renew.

The Light came into darkness,
To shine through all we do.

The Light, illuminates and guides us,
As we go on our way.

We thank our Heavenly Father,
For the Light of Christ this Day!

Christmas Joy

May the Joy of Christmas fill your heart,
As the story unfolds and you play a part.

May you experience the Joy and Peace from above,
And hearts aglow with warmth and love.

May God's love abound with Jesus birth,
As you witness God, come down to earth.

In the form of a child, a gift beyond measure,
God's promised Son, our true hearts' treasure.

Jesus' Birth

Moonlight glow and shining star,
We focus on a land so far.

There, in tiny manger bed,
Our Lord Jesus laid his head.

Joseph and Mary's blessed event,
Jesus, the Son of God, was sent.

Creatures gathered great and small,
To pay tribute, to them all.

Shepherds heard the angels sing,
Praises to the new born king.

Wisemen guided from afar,
With the shining of a star.

The "Prince of Peace" is born today,
All did humbly bow to pray.

Angels sang of Jesus' birth,
Peace shall blanket all the earth.

God Sent

God sent a child,
To change a life.
The life of all,
Who were in strife.

God sent a child,
To bless us all.
To bring us to Him, and
save us from the fall.

God sent a child,
To show the way,
We need to Love,
Each other today.

A precious Child,
A gift from above.
A special child,
To us with Love.

Jesus is Born

Stars like diamonds in the sky,
Brought the Angels from on high.

As the shepherds watched and stood in fear,
Being told the Son of God was near.

Search for him the Angels said.
A babe wrapped in cloths in manger bed.

The angels' chorus loud and clear,
With words for shepherds all to hear.

"Glory to God in the Highest" they sang,
And " Peace to Men", the voices rang.

To Bethlehem the shepherds went,
To find the Son of God, been sent.

With Mary, Joseph and Babe so dear,
It was to be known the message was clear.

Jesus was here,
The Son of God born,
On this special night,
With angels adorn.

So, we give God Glory,
We sing God's Praise,
We thank God for Jesus,
All of our Days.

A Dark Road to Life

Lord,
With tear-filled eyes,
I watch the strap,
As it rips Your flesh.

Like tiny swords,
The crown of thorns
Pierces Your head.

As You trod the dusty road to death,
Bent is Your frame, My Lord,
Overshadowed by the weight of the cross.

I fall to my knees,
My heart screaming out.
But no words pass these lips,
Just tear-streaked cheeks.

"Don't leave me!", my heart cries out.
As You surrender Your Spirit to Your Father in Heaven.

Darkness replaces the day,
And there is mourning and wailing on the Hill.

But, Light replaces darkness,
And Joy replaces our sorrow,
And the day dawns anew.

For the King of Kings has Risen,
He is victorious over sin and death.
He is Alive, with us and Among us,
Now and Forever!

Eastertide

When the golden sun
Begins to rise,

We see the
Blueness of the skies,

And Hallelujahs we
Start to sing,

For Christ is risen,
Our Savior, King!

The truth of God's
Undying Love,

He claims His children,
From up above,

And by His mercy,
And Abiding Grace,

God meets His children,
Face to Face!

King of Kings

Sing a song of Joyfulness,
The Son of Him above.

Who came down from the heavens,
And died for those He Loved.

Sing a Song of Gratefulness,
Hosanna's loud and strong,
For our Savior,
King of Kings,
Who sits upon His throne.

Rejoice ye Servant,
Leap Ye Lame,
Repent, Sinner we employ,

The Lord has come,
The King of Kings,
Rejoice and leap for Joy!

The cross remains;
A trilogy of God,
The 3-In-One,
Father, Holy Spirit and Jesus Christ the Son!

SPECIAL OCCASIONS

Happy Mother's Day

If I could bring you flowers,
To brighten up your day,

And shower you with blessings,
As you go on your way,

If I could bring you happiness,
And joyful moments too,

Then I'd be very happy,
Celebrating the wonderfulness
Of You!

Mother, Did You Know?

Mother did you know...
I'd never walk without you?

Mother did you ever think…
I'd take wing and fly?

Mother did you know.
Your legacy would linger?

Mother did you think...
Time would pass you by?

Mother did you know…
Your Love would live forever…

In the hearts of children…
You weaned so long ago?

Mother did you know…
You'd found a hidden treasure?

After all your searching…
In the hearts that love you so!

Mother/Child

Gently held to Mother's breast,
Mother rocks her child to rest.

Precious gift of God's own giving,
Tiny life, miracle of living.

God bless this child with, mother's care,
Mother's nurturing abiding there.

Tender gift from God above,
Surrounded by a world of Love.

Mother/Child sweet and tender,
Bring about the lives we render.

A special bond established at birth,
Little child with unmeasurable worth.

Mother with love unsurpassing,
A relationship that's everlasting.

Of God's own making, this gift from above,
A Mother/Child wrapped up in love.

We Are Proud

For thy honor, We all stand.
Hand to hand Across this land.
Lifting up the Red, White and Blue,
Stating We are proud of You!

You who defend and keep us free,
Safe from terror, insanity.

Safe to be, whoever we be.

People who speak, what's on their mind,
Other who are not so kind.

People who can worship as we dare,
Knowing we can anywhere.

So thankful we are to those who fight,
To protect our country and our right,

To live our lives and know you're there,
Fighting for all, you deeply care.

To fight a war on Terror and Fear,
So that someday "Peace" may be near.

A high price to pay, many lives may be lost,
But, people will know, freedom comes at great cost.

And when it is over and our heroes come back,
They will see it's not support that they lack.

Colors flying high of the Red, White and Blue,
And yellow ribbons tied round our trees too,
In support of their efforts, and all that they do,
Sending a message, "We're Proud of You!"

The Relationship

The time has come,
For me to go,

Just want to say,
"I Love You, So".

I've carried you within,
My heart, We've really,
Never been apart.

Though miles separated,
Me from you,
I've treasured visits,
That renew.

A relationship.
Like none other,
The relationship,
Of Son and Mother.

(Dedicated to Rich in memory of his mother, Betty Delores Benson Hartlieb)

You're Part of Me

You became part of my life,
You remain that today.

Precious gifts from above,
You're remembered that way.

I'll keep in touch and remain a part,
For your life's been woven in my heart.

Try not to be sad,
A change was due.

Look to tomorrow,
To the exciting and new.

Dream your dreams!
Take a chance!
Live your Life!
Dance the Dance!

A Shared Union

Share a love, share a life,
Share the bond husband/wife.

Fill a dream, shared in Love,
With God's Blessing from above.

Share the good and share the bad,
For God is there, rejoice. Be glad.

Offer up your gifts and praise,
He will bless you all your days.

As you continue a life of bliss,
Just take time, remember this;

God is with you throughout your life,
As you continue man and wife.

Live for the Lord, a life of care,
For each and everyone be there.

A special union, Christ hath bless,
Continue in your happiness.

And may your days, continue to be,
Filled with the Love of Christ, in thee.

(Written in Celebration of Maureen and Howard's 25th Wedding Anniversary)

Words Never Spoken

A grateful heart of thankfulness,
To all of those who care.

Your warmth and prayers of healing,
Show me you're always there.

Hospitality, encouragement you have
Given along the way.

Your presence in the notes you send
Make a much brighter day.

I really feel so truly blessed,
To have such friends as you.

With God and you attending me,
There's nothing I can't do.

And so, again with grateful heart,
There's just one more thing to say

I Love My Family at Scottsville Church,
God's blessed me with this day.

(Written as a poem of thanks to my Scottsville Church Family)

Open Us To Music

Open us to music,
Around us everyday,
The chirping of the birds,
The children as they play.

Open us to music,
Church bells in distance call,
And people gather in,
To worship Lord of All.

Open us to music,
And open us to the word,
Hidden in its beauty,
There's a message to be heard.

Open us to music,
May the Spirit touch our soul,
And in our Praise and Worship,
We will be made whole!

(dedicated to Anita Walton, director of music, Scottsville United Methodist Church 2007)

Service In The Lord

(to the tune of "Jesus Loves Me")

We're commissioned to the world,
Telling all of God's true word.

He sent Jesus, from above,
To come to earth to show His love.

Chorus:
Love calls to action (3x's)
Don't sit Idle, by!

Jesus said "come follow Me",
Spirit filled you'll be set free,

Follow service in the Lord,
In Him your life will be restored.

Chorus:
We're called to service (3x's)
We can't sit idle, by!

(Hymn of Mission written at School Of Missions 2007)

About the Author

Maureen S. Birkett, A writer of Christian Poetry, was born and raised, and continues to live in the outskirts of Northeast Philadelphia, Pennsylvania in a little town called Oakford. Maureen has a Faith that is deeply rooted in our Lord, Jesus Christ; a Faith that has helped her cope with life's difficulties: raising a handicapped child, dealing with the pain of Fibromyalgia, and handling the problems associated with parenthood. She has a very supportive husband who is always there for her. She loves her family.

She is a Christ Servant Minister in her home church of Scottsville United Methodist Church in Langhorne. Maureen has a passion for writing poetry, and enjoying music as displayed by her involvement in the Sanctuary, Praise and Worship, Youth, and Bell Choirs. Maureen has shared her love of poetry with her Scottsville Family and has done poetry readings for her grandaughter's elementary school.

She enjoys working with young people with special needs. She teaches a special needs Sunday School Class and youth group, which meets at her church on Sunday Evenings from September through May.

She Loves the Lord and gives thanks to Him for her many talents. This is the first of her hopefully, many books Glorifying God!